AN AFFAIR

The First 90 Days After Discovery

This book is written to help you through the initial paralyzing shock and confusion so difficult decisions can be made, and your path to healing and recovery can begin

November 1, 2024

Linda M. Price, PhD, Psychotherapist

Linda0331@icloud.com

A new day is upon you. Perhaps this day will be the day that everything changes and healing begins.

I want to thank each and every couple and individual I've met along this journey who showed me healing and recovery are possible after an Affair. I also want to thank all those who encouraged me to write this book, and gave me the freedom of hours upon hours to prepare this book just for "you" who is reading it. Thank you ....

Linda M. Price, Psychotherapist, PhD

Table of Contents

Hello, and thank you for choosing my book to help you through what most describe as one of the more painful and traumatic times of

their lives.

In deciding how to write this book about recovery from Affairs, I decided the most beneficial way was to speak with you as though you were right here in my office. Many of the suggestions I will bring up, or examples I mention, I have witnessed in my own therapy practice.   I wish I could say that this book of step-by-step recovery will be easy, but unfortunately, it is not. There will be a lot that will be asked of the person who Betrayed you, and there will be a lot asked of the person who has been Betrayed. This is not a book of blame or shame. This is not a book where I will demonize the person who has Betrayed their partner. Rather, it is to help you reclaim your sense of self-confidence, peace of mind, and a plan to determine your next decisions.

This book is written to help you not only through the first 90 days after discovery, but the continuing changes needed to rebuild the marriage if that is what both of you want to do.

This book is also written from the perspective of someone who has witnessed the incredible miracle of recovery, and as one client told me "Dr. Price, if I had not tried to find a way to go beyond the pain in my heart and find a way through mutual effort to build a new relationship, I would not see the "miracles" I'm witnessing today." This is why I keep helping couples heal …. for themselves, for their families, for their children and their future.

I have many couples coming to me before reading my book, and they -- more often than not -- say "I wish I had come to you first". There are fundamental things that need to happen and fundamental things that need not happen. Most people have no road map when it comes to an
Affair, and their first instinct is to "scorch the earth". I need to say here – that really does not help you at all. It may give a moment of celebration, a moment of inner silence from your rage and hatred,

but it will not last. The old saying warns: "Hanging on to

bitterness, hatred and rage is like drinking your own poison and

expecting the other person to die".

I will take you through my own program of recovery which

includes the Critical Stage of the First 90 Days, the Acute Stage

and the

Healing and Recovery Stage

But first, let me share some of the truths about recovery from Affairs through my program, and let me share with you a little about myself. While I use the term "relationship" in this book, that term applies to marriages as well as long-term and short-term relationships

I am a licensed Marriage and Family Therapist, a certified Guided

Imagery Therapist, hold a PhD in Holistic Counseling, and I am a Gottman trained couples' therapist. I also am a Christian who believes in the power of faith to help you through this difficult time.

I have spent over 20+ years helping couples recover from Affairs and other challenging mental conditions. I have devoted the majority of my practice to understanding and learning from my couples what it takes to recover from an Affair, and I now want to pass on their wisdom and truths to you.

I am also speaking to you from my own perspective as one who experienced an Affair in my first marriage. I can't say if we had used what I know now, we would have recovered. All I know is that I am now in a loving relationship with someone I adore and trust completely. We are celebrating over 20 years together, and I feel so blessed.

I do believe and have witnessed that relationships can recover from even the most hurtful Affairs. By trusting in God's guidance during my sessions and by believing that recovery is possible, I offer Hope to each of my couples for a better future.

Unfortunately, sometimes relationships can't be saved. I wish they could, but for some the healing process is just too painful and for some they know they will never get over it and would spend the rest of their years punishing the Betrayer, and by punishing the Betrayer, they are also punishing themselves.

So, by punishing the Betrayer, nothing goes forward, and the pain continues. What kind of life would that be? To feel you just could not ever forgive the Betrayer. In my opinion, it is a gift of kindness to let the person go and in return let yourself go from the agony of the Affair and move forward in life.

The first couple I ever dealt with was when I was an Intern and not even licensed but getting my hours to be licensed….and I was awful. I pushed them too fast and too hard, but through them, I learned so much about the determination of a couple to keep a relationship and rebuild.

I felt defeated by my inexperience. I had never in all my years of education been guided in how to help such a serious situation. So, I started researching, I started listening to people who recovered and I started becoming more aware of the devastation of an Affair. This couple had so much trust in me, and they continued to come to our sessions. Over a period of one year, we were able to get to the healing part of recovery, and after so many years, I still hear from them. They have gone on to have a successful relationship and are enjoying the family they once wondered if they would ever have.

This experience taught me that healing and recovery can occur …. but not always.

I wish I could guarantee by using the principles I mention in this book, you will recover and all will be okay. But I can't do that. I can only share what I have learned and witnessed to allow the best chance for recovery. I have seen incredible recoveries from using these simple principles. I have also seen some people unable to recover. I understand that some hurts "are not forgivable".

I do understand your pain and feel true empathy for what you are going through. Even though I do not know your name, I honestly do know your circumstances. Search your heart and soul and determine if you honestly feel the relationship is worth saving – are you and your relationship partner ready for the challenging work, the hours, days and months of working toward recovery? I hope so.

I wish you all the best.

What is considered an Affair: I've been asked this question many times. I think we all know when there is a physical Affair, where sexual encounters are part of the Affair it is easy to identify this type of relationship as an Affair. Whether it is a one-night stand or weeks, months, or years of meeting each other, this is an Affair.

But what about those "innocent" flirtations, those lunches where only work is talked about, but then personal information begins to be shared, or trips where there are separate rooms, but all other times are spent together: meetings, outings, seminars, lunches, dinners, etc.

Would this be considered an Affair?

What about work that consumes one person where there is absolutely no time for your partner. Work becomes obsessive, where the person receives all their "emotional support" from being around and involved in the work environment. Or…is there a hobby that takes all the time away from nourishing and supporting each other?

It is my belief, after working with many, many couples, that "an Affair" can be determined by how much emotional and/or physical energy is given to something or someone who is not your partner. Where personal information is shared about numerous things…. how you feel about something, what challenges you are going through, and most important, the person looks forward to discussing all of this with that person rather than the person you have declared your loyalty too. The person may actually look forward to "escaping" to their work environment solely for the emotional benefit it provides.

As I have advised many couples: Imagine your partner is standing right beside you. If you are doing something that would cause hurt or humiliation to your partner, you need to rethink what you are doing.   I once had a couple come in and the male partner was buying expensive gifts for a woman at work "who needed his help". He went so far as to buy her a very expensive gift. He did not believe he was doing anything wrong and described her as only a "friend". The wife was confused and emotionally distraught and I felt so deeply sorry for her. In discussing this "friendship" further, I suggested that perhaps his wife could be included in some of the lunches and dinners he was having with his "friend". He became so angry with me for even suggesting this, he got up, threw some papers at me, walked out while slamming the door so hard that ceiling tiles were coming down. This is an emotional Betrayal of the highest order. I think he knew it was an Affair but did not want his wife to get confirmation from anyone that it was an Affair. She felt better by being validated for her concerns. He refused to continue therapy.

I hope this helps in determining the existence of an Affair. Do not lower your bar of emotional security so far down that all behaviors are acceptable. It only breeds distrust, isolation, and distance between two people. Now let's go forward…

The Beginning

Do You Stay or Leave

This is asked immediately. I wish I had proven guidelines to advise you one way or the other, but I do not. I can only state that separation and divorce are very individual decisions.

I do advise my couples to not make an especially life-changing decision based on their emotional state alone. I have found with most couples that when the decision to leave or divorce is made purely on the emotions felt at the moment, there can possibly be a time when regret moves in. I'm not stating that is always the case, but it does happen.   When a separation takes place it sends an alarm to your children, family and friends that something unrecoverable has happened and now what will life look like. Who chooses who in the friendship category, and most importantly, how will the children wrap their heads around one person who is no longer present?

So perhaps take a long weekend away from each other or visit a

friend or family member for a few days and allow yourself to have

the freedom to feel what you need to do without the negative

energy of the Affair around you. I do encourage that this be a time

of deep reflection, not a time to discuss the facts of the Affair. I

call it a "silent mental and emotional retreat" – one that allows you

to think without mental "noise" to discover what you want to do.

For me, my perfect place is the mountains which reminds me

of strength and safety. Maybe for you, it is in the mountains or at

the ocean   Wherever you feel the most able to connect with what

you can accept, and not accept, will be exactly where you need to

be. Once you return, perhaps you will have a better understanding

and a better picture of the decision you need to make.

The Pain -- When Does It End

You are deeply wounded, and there is no quick fix to this

emotional trauma. It will completely consume you in the beginning,

but there is Hope that this trauma can be healed.   If there is no

"Hope" at the moment, I understand. It is hard to call upon Hope when all around you seems hopeless.

To get beyond the initial trauma of the Affair will take an incredible "Leap of Faith" that you will recover and that this pain you are feeling now will fade over time. You will also be asked to "Lay down your Sword" of moral superiority so that you can once again be "you".

There is a blanket of hurt and pain weighing you down now, but you can learn to remove this emotional blanket of pain, humiliation, and shock so you can breathe freely.

To lessen the pain, there must be an acknowledgement of the powerful explosion in your brain and heart that brings unbelievable shock to the Betrayed person's life. It is a terrible emotional roller coaster ride…anger turns to depression which in turn returns to anger and rage, and it goes on and on. You may feel this for some time until the ride comes to an end.

There is an understanding in therapy that it could take at least 2 years before complete trust is rebuilt. For some of my clients, it was a much shorter time, but for others, I am still seeing them on occasion several years later. This does not mean you would be in therapy for two years, but that the journey to healing can sometimes take that long.

My sole purpose in authoring this book is to help you get to that place of whatever it is that feels right to you…. peace, understanding, forgiveness, trust, separation, divorce. It is a difficult road you are traveling on now, and all the choices are open to you.

In the many years I have counseled couples, there has not been one person who has sought my help who didn't express "No one will believe this", "I don't believe this", "I would never believe he or she would cheat on me" These are some of the statements I most often hear from my clients.
It is this blindsided shock that shakes us to our very soul.

Likewise, there has never been a couple come to me and say, "my partner just shared with me….". Never. It is always "I found out accidentally when I picked up the phone and there was a message from a person that was suspicious", or "I felt something was going on and I started looking for evidence". The shock of being blindsided by this information is a gut punch and the world as we knew it changes forever.

The pain will begin to lessen as you work through your feelings and you and your partner create a new relationship from its ashes. The next question usually is about whether the pain and uncertainty will last forever …. I hope for you it does leave you, and that the pain transforms both of you so you can create a new and healthy relationship.

There may be a day or a week or months down the road that you don't think about it and even must remind yourself of what you went through, but that is down the road.

If there is anything at all you haven't shared about the Affair, please tell all now. Here's one of my stories about not telling all:

In helping a couple many years, the person who caused the Affair was completely involved in rebuilding the relationship, but the person Betrayed felt something was still off. I encouraged both parties to continue therapy and allow new rituals and behaviors to develop. We were in our fourth month of therapy when the discovery was made that the Affair was never ended. Crushing information that ended the relationship immediately. They both got up and walked out. I heard the next day that papers for a divorce were filed that morning.

The reason I'm pointing this out to the person who Betrayed is that you have one shot and one shot only to share everything. The consequences are yours to shoulder and it's best for everything to be known at the beginning of healing. Most people tell me they don't want to hurt their partner anymore, but the hurt is already done, the trauma has already been experienced. Pain and suffering can be worked through, but finding out the Affair did not end when trust is being developed is devastating beyond words I can write here.

The relationship is literally in ashes …. Let's not do anything more to hurt the person Betrayed. Don't ask for trust, and then sabotage the trust down the road. It's disastrous!

It is the very beginning of rebuilding trust through transparency, and it is essential. In fact, whatever the Betrayed partner needs …. e.g., looking at phone, text messages, emails …. anything that will help the Betrayed person regain a sense of safety and peace should be encouraged and accepted by the person who has caused the Affair.

I've had some tell me "It isn't fair that their personal information would be available whenever needed by the Betrayed partner". I have to remind them that they lost the privilege of holding personal information private when they crossed the line into infidelity, secrets and lying.

The Betrayer can't express any excuse for the Affair. For your partner to be told you are sorry only to follow it with "but……." never, and I will repeat, never will help. No matter your "excuse", no matter the circumstances that put you in a place to Betray, you alone made the decision to cross the line into infidelity, and you alone will bear the burden of the consequences. If there are other circumstances or if there are unresolved problems in the relationship that need to be addressed, then do that when some healing has taken place. To put the Betrayed partner in a position of accepting any type of responsibility for the Affair is just deliberately causing more pain and suffering. It is cruel and will indefinitely delay healing.

End the Affair Relationship.

The first and most crucial step in the beginning stages of an Affair is that the person who has committed the Affair MUST end all communication and connection with the other person. No more text messages, phone calls, emails, or any other type of communication whether in person or through other means.

If the Betrayed person wants to witness your untangling yourself from the Affair partner, I would strongly suggest you allow that to happen. If you cut off the other person before your Betrayed partner is allowed to witness this happen, you will have to do it all over again because the Betrayed partner must be a part of this initial process.

If the Betrayed partner wants to witness all cut-off of communication with the other person, remember -- It is their "day in court" so to speak. They get to face the person who has caused so much harm and they get to ask questions and express to this person their profound anger, including how this act of Betrayal has destroyed the foundation of the relationship and the family. In this way, it allows the Betrayed person to regain some control over this situation and begin to rebuild their self-respect and self-confidence.

One other important part of this is that they get to verify what you have already told them about the Affair. Without stating the obvious, I do hope you have shared all the facts of the Affair.

Who do you tell:

It is important to keep all the details of the Affair between the two of you. I do suggest that if there is one person who you trust completely to share this information, then do that. However, now is not the time to spread to every member of your family and your friends what has happened. They will forever change their opinion of the Betrayer, and possibly even you. As you start to rebuild your relationship, these individuals will not know the demanding work that you both have done and will still be back where they first learned of the Affair.

When there is absolutely no hope for the future of the relationship and divorce is on the table, then it is time to share and request their support as you go through this most challenging time.

As time goes on and you have decided it is worth it to rebuild the relationship, you may want to share this information with valued members of your family and friends. By delaying telling the information in the beginning you are given an opportunity to not only tell what happened, but also share what you both have learned and achieved in working through the beginning stage of healing.

The Children:

This is tough. Children never want their parents to have trouble and there is an unspoken fear that some children carry of "what if" my parents go through what Olive's parents went through or Joe's parents or even, Aunt Susie or Uncle Paul. They hear it among friends and if they are in school, they certainly hear it there.

There is also the unspoken truth in children that if Daddy or Mommy fall out of love and want to end their relationship and move out or away, can that happen to them as well? Can Mommy and/or Daddy one day not love us enough to stay? Will one of them leave? A child's brain is too immature and underdeveloped to sort out the real-life issues of grown adults. This can lead to a child becoming hypervigilant about being "perfect" so their parents will always love them and never leave.

I hope you can see that how you manage discussing the Affair has many levels to it, especially for children.

If you must say something because your child has asked a question, please reassure them all will be okay. Then be sure to ask them what they are thinking about. Give them an opportunity to share with you their feelings and worries. Remember – a child lays their little head on the pillow at night and there is no one for them to turn to and ask for comfort.
It is your primary job to make sure they feel safe and secure.

So, hold off on discussing with the children what is going on with the two of you. Even if you have adult children…. just wait. These are grown-up issues that do not require their attention or input.

How Much Detail Do You Really Want to Know:

Most people who have been Betrayed will ask a lot of questions, and some of these questions may center around a moment-by-moment description of everything that happened. The Betrayed person may pull out a calendar and match up dates with incongruities in times away from each other, or broken dates or events with family or friends.   All I ask is that you ask yourself "do I really want to know all the details". Once the information is said, there is no way to forget that detail. So, I encourage my clients to ask questions about:

(1) how were you different in the Affair,

(2) did you think of me,

(3) and if you did, what were your thoughts

(4) was it hard to lie to me,

(5) did you think of the children, etc.

Any questions along these lines to understand on a deeper level the

Betrayer's state of mind is essential.

However, most people ask all the questions and then come to me to help them process the "mental images" they carry around from the answers to the questions. Again….do you really want to know the answers, and can you live the rest of your life with the answers.

I want to remind you …. You did nothing wrong; you are a person deserving of respect and honesty, and you are stronger, more beautiful/handsome, more intelligent and more loving than the "other person". You did not fail….

How Often Do You Discuss the Affair:

Marathon discussions about an Affair are exhausting and literally cause you more harm than good. They also keep real discussions at bay. It takes so much energy to engage in these types of discussions – I've had clients who spent all night, the next day and the next week arguing over the details of the Affair and the hurt that it has caused without any amount of understanding or empathy being displayed.

It will not move the two of you forward to what decisions need to be made about the relationship. The same things are said, the same responses are heard, the same feelings are being felt. Again, it saddens my heart when I have a couple come in the office with blood shot eyes, looking like death warmed over and desperately trying to find the courage and strength to go on because they have engaged in yet another marathon yelling match.

Yes, there needs to be discussion, but what I encourage my clients to do is set aside daily a time of 15-20 minutes (more or less) to discuss the

Affair. This will give each person a chance to "reset" the brain, to evaluate just what is needed to be said, and it will help discipline your emotions. I do not believe this happens naturally. It takes practice and patience. I have couples who have shared with me they were having a good time together, feeling more relaxed and hopeful, only to be blindsided at that moment with a remark about the Affair. It takes away a moment of building "good feelings" and it throws both people back into feelings of despair. If both of you know there will be a time later in the day to discuss the Affair, the process of disciplining the mind to delay gratification and to reassure yourself the issues will be discussed can begin. This guarantees to the Betrayed person the Affair will not be just swept under the rug and their anxiety and stress can be reduced.

This does not mean you have to deny what you are feeling at the moment. You can certainly express that "this time of day, this place we are visiting, etc., is making it difficult for me to enjoy this moment." Then ask from your partner what you need to feel comfortable.

I also suggest if there is something particularly good that has happened, or you have noticed a beginning softening, please share that.

Success breeds success even in recovery from Affairs, and you both need to hear it is getting better.

I had one couple who would read scripture to each other before each discussion and another who would read a motivational quote, and yet another who would request an "agenda" of what was to be talked about. Whatever works for you, that is what you need to use, and you can certainly experiment with what works best. Try different ideas and those that work best, then stick to them. There is not one right thing to do because everyone is unique in their own journey.

There is a lot of energy in your home right now and most of it is negative. That is why I encourage my couples to try out different places to discuss the Affair. To continually go back to the same room, in the same chairs at the same time only fosters a feeling of dread…it's like constantly returning to the scene of the crime to discuss it one more time. Give space to your discussions…. go outside if you can, go for a walk, or whatever seems better for you.

Social Events. I have discovered by counselling my couples that social events are by far the most difficult to manage.

It is a reminder of what they don't have anymore, and it becomes hard to disguise exactly what is going on in the relationship. If possible, keep social events to a minimum or not at all. I understand if certain events are necessary or even mandatory and I encourage you to think it is only a brief time not forever you need to act "normal". You may be utterly exhausted after one of these events and I encourage you to rest. Take time to allow your emotional state to have a moment of peace and serenity.

Please discuss before the social event how you will both interact with each other. Do you need to stand together, is it okay to hold hands, is it okay to touch at all? Perhaps you need to be close to each other and that's okay. Perhaps you both set a time for how long you will stay. Whatever is needed to set the requirements for the social event, please discuss them prior to going.

Self-Care. An Affair like the one you are experiencing is the same as responding to a traumatic event. It comes with an almost

desperate need to self-isolate to protect yourself from further

emotional harm.

The effects of experiencing a traumatic event as described in a Google

Search and displayed by Home-Bay Road Counseling (Home - Bay Road

Counselling (bayroadcounsellingandpsychology.com.au)) are as follows:

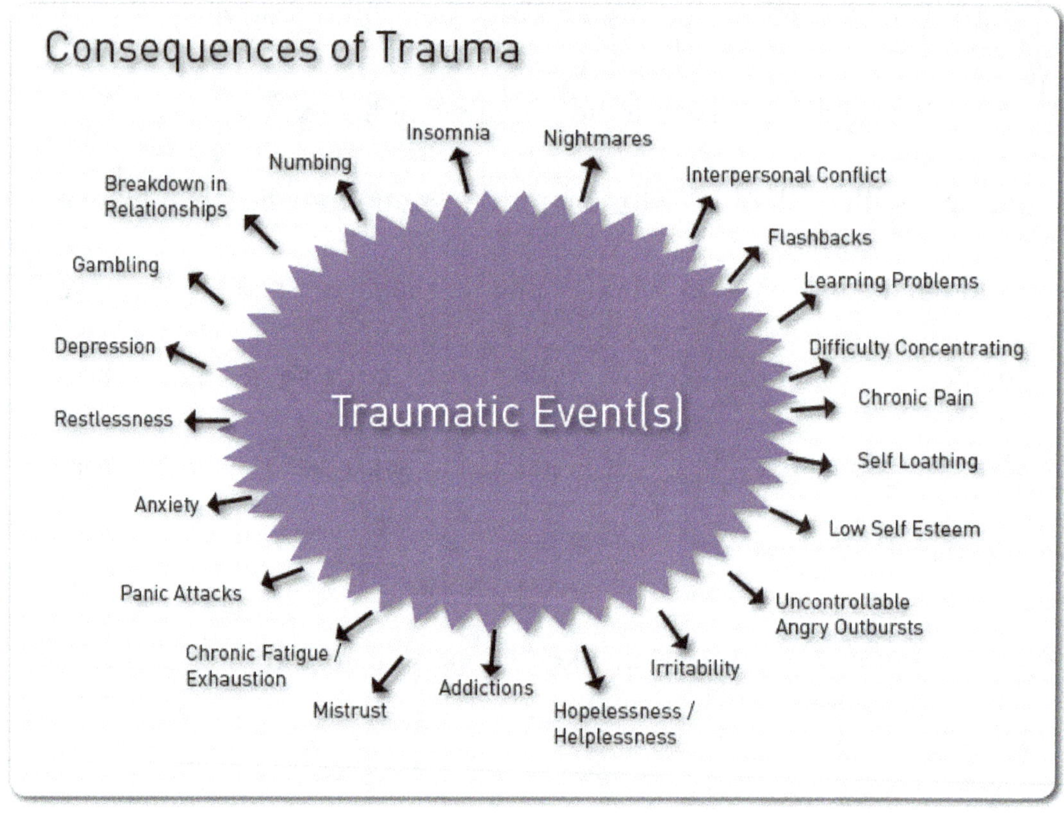

If you can identify with some of these symptoms, you may also be experiencing what is termed a "Flight, Fight or Freeze" response. As described by Web MD on a Google Search:

"**What Is Fight or Flight?**

In fight or flight mode, your brain is preparing for a physical response.

Fight. When your body feels that it is in danger and believes you can overpower the threat, you'll respond in fight mode. Your brain releases signals to your body, preparing it for the physical demands of fighting.

Signs of a fight response include:

- Tight jaw

- Grinding your teeth

- Urge to punch something or someone

- A feeling of intense anger

- Need to stomp or kick

- Crying in anger

- A burning or knotted sensation in your stomach

- Attacking the source of danger

Flight. If your body believes you cannot overcome the danger but can avoid it by running away, you'll respond in flight mode. A surge of hormones, like **adrenaline**, give your body the stamina to run from danger longer than you typically could.

Signs of a flight response include:

- Excessive exercising

- Feeling fidgety, tense, or trapped

- Constantly moving your legs, feet, and arms

- Restless body

- Feeling of numbness in your arms and legs

- Dilated or darting eyes."

-

Freeze. This stress response causes you to feel stuck in place. This response happens when your body does not think you can fight or flight.

Signs of the freeze response include

- Sense of dread
- Pale skin
- Feeling stiff, heavy, cold, and numb
- Loud, pounding heart
- Decreasing heart rate"

As shown by the above chart, a traumatic event is far from easy to overcome. You may feel surreal, that your life is a jumbled puzzle, and you can't seem to find the right pieces to put it back together.

That's why as difficult as it may be in the beginning stages of recovery, it is also especially important and necessary to focus on your own self-care.

If you have neglected your self-care, and not included it in your daily routine, now is the time to start. Whatever you decide to do is perfect…..just determine to put yourself first. .

Are you eating and sleeping properly? Are you taking care of your hygiene…bathing, brushing your teeth and all the other things that we need to do to feel good about ourselves. If you feel very depressed, are you seeking assistance?

Depression is a silent disturber of your inner peace. You may find the bed is more inviting than everyday functioning, but I want to encourage you to develop a routine that consciously ignores the escape to the bed.

Through therapy, meditation or medications or a combination of all three, you can find relief from the symptoms of the trauma. It does not mean you will need this forever but if these things help, please include them.

If you can make some time to go outside daily, the benefits will be felt immediately. Many studies have proven that being outside in nature provides emotional healing and allows the brain to have a "mental vacation" from all the turmoil. Even 10-20 minutes of being outside will be beneficial. Fresh air, looking at nature or engaging in any type of outdoor activity relaxes our thoughts and allows our brain to feel free of the trauma – if only for a while.

Family Gatherings.

If you live close to family, perhaps family gatherings are routine and weekly. It may be incredibly difficult to disguise that all is okay around people who know you all too well. As with what I suggested for social events, the same guidelines hold true for family

gatherings as well. I suggest before each gathering you both decide

how you will handle the family event – will you stand with each

other, will you hold hands, will touching at all be permissible, what

will you offer as explanation if asked if anything is wrong, what is

the energy you will be displaying.

Try to make it as easy for both of you as possible. Whatever

you decide to do is right…. there are no rights or wrongs when it

comes to events such as these.

Work Trips

Many times, one or both partners must travel for their job. This

can be especially difficult after the initial discovery of the Affair,

especially if the Affair happened on a work trip. There may be a

decision to ask for exclusion from any work trips until a sense of

stability and safety in the relationship has occurred.

For the Betrayed partner, discuss with your partner what you need to feel connected and safe. Text, Facetime, Zoom, email, accompanying your partner on the trip. Think about what would make you feel less anxiety and more comfortable with your partner leaving.

During this time, the person who has Betrayed needs to be especially attentive to your partner's needs. Before you leave, talk with your partner about what is needed and be aware of little "gifts of kindness" that you can leave behind for your partner to find.

By "little gifts of kindness" be mindful of what your partner likes the most. In other words, your partner's love language.

According to Chapman (1992) "Your emotional love language and the language of your spouse may be as different as Chinese and English".

His book entitled "The Five Love Languages" helps identify what each partner in a relationship needs. You may think you know what your partner likes to feel safe and loved, but this book allows you and your partner to think beyond what you "think you know". I

recommend this to all my couples. It has been around for many years

and helped many couples identify their own "love language".

Innocence and Blind Trust Are Destroyed

It is at this stage that you realize that the innocence and blind

trust of this incredible relationship have been severely damaged, if not

destroyed.

Death comes to us in many different scenarios.   I think we

know the most common gut-wrenching ones…the loss of a parent or

best

friend, the loss of a child, the loss of a loyal pet, the loss of a job, the

loss of a tomorrow we believed we had ……but an Affair is also like

a death, especially the death of innocence and blind trust in your

relationship.

You cannot bring back innocence – it is a once in a lifetime feeling

for a relationship. But trust can be rebuilt. Through transparency, authenticity and genuine remorse and truth telling, trust can slowly and gradually come back to life.

But what is innocence? I don't mean the kind of our childhood youth…it is more a relationship where conflict has been resolved, communication is open and honest and where true regard for the other person is shown daily. It is a relationship with arguments, agreements, forgiveness, laughter, hidden flirtations with each other and secrets between each other that no one else knows about, it is a relationship that is solidly built on a foundation of trust, loyalty, and fidelity to each other, it is a relationship that has a distinct, forever future. A picture of old age with children and grandchildren and maybe a once in a lifetime trip or sitting on a front porch, drinking tea or whatever you like, rocking in a rocking chair and waiting for grandchildren to come over. It is the best kind of relationship, and you were living it……

But…. It was not a relationship envisioned with an Affair. The "innocence" of the relationship has now been broken and has blurred your vision of what the future will be like, or if there will be a future at all with the person who Betrayed you.

This type of loss is intense. When you were the most vulnerable and transparent and felt the most secure, it was at this time, you were Betrayed. How will you trust again, be vulnerable again or even feel a sense of peace again. I have heard all these questions and concerns over the years, and it still breaks my heart when I see someone look at me for answers. How do we turn doubt into trust, trust into believing again and believing again into peace and comfort in your heart.

It is accomplished through what I can only describe as a "Leap of Faith". What exactly is that: Well, it is gambling on the idea that trust can be rebuilt, that hurt will be healed and that this type of Betrayal will never happen again. That is a lot to ask, and as I stated above, it takes a big

"Leap of Faith". However, the gamble is based not on sheer innocence that all "will be okay" because that is gone, but rather it will be based on new behaviors, new rituals, and new understandings about the sacredness of the relationship.

It is a gamble of your emotional well-being that even though what has happened to you has been devastating, you are willing to accept the repairs of the Betrayer and allow trust to be built again. That's a lot to ask, isn't it? Let me reassure you this does not happen overnight. It takes small increments of trust building to take place. It takes patience. It takes a lot of heart, and it takes all your mental and emotional strength to tackle this every single day. I'm trying not to sugar coat on purpose because the journey can be a difficult one.

So, what if you have no faith that anything will improve…. that is okay too. Your desire to pick up this book, to reach out for understanding is proof of your desire to "know" what happened and to understand the undeniable truths in your relationship…. There were hurts, disappointments, irritations and a host of other things that were not discussed, and if they were discussed, nothing ever changed.

Keeping the peace or "accepting" rather than confronting became the norm. But you might say…. We never argued, we never treated each other badly. I want to suggest to you the possibility that that statement is not entirely true.

Silence is also a powerful way to communicate. In fact, in my opinion and from what I have witnessed, "silence" and "throwing everything under the rug to just ignore" are the most destructive coping behaviors in a relationship. To have to use the energy it takes to stay in this state in a relationship is devastating to your mental, physical, emotional, and spiritual health.   It only brings about a host of other problems, including anxiety, depression, nervousness, physical ailments, and a desire to not "rock the boat". "Walking on eggshells" becomes normal and necessary to not upset the façade of "everything is okay" at the present moment. Better to ignore than to confront? Is that your relationship?

But ignoring only makes the problem bigger, the ability to discuss issues even more difficult, and the false sense that all is "right" tolerable   I'm so saddened sometimes at what couples will endure and use as the "bar" for acceptable behaviors for their relationship. It is so low that almost any undesirable behavior is acceptable. The low bar has been necessary though. It prevents massive arguments, periods of harsh words and treatment, and it keeps everyone incredibly on edge but "safe" in a strange kind of way.   There may not be an outward display of stress, but inward, there may be a lot going on. I'm going to ask you to raise that bar. To allow honest and open communication and to again "put down your sword" and find new ways to allow freedom of expression and freedom of feelings in your relationship. It is hard, but it can be done.

What Are Triggers and How Can They Be Minimized

A normal day, sounds, time of day, a meal you were enjoying, activity you were engaged in, and a host of other things are all Triggers that surround the person who has been Betrayed.   From looking at a phone, to driving down a street, to just looking at the person who has Betrayed you.

These triggers may throw you back into the exact feeling you had when you first found out.

I teach my clients from Cognitive Behavior Therapy coping skills that (1) what we think becomes (2) what we feel. and then (3) determines the behaviors we use. So, if what we think puts us in a tailspin, controlling our thoughts will begin to help us, right   the problem becomes how does a person control their thoughts since thoughts are random. It is not easy, but by reframing the thought as one that is not catastrophic but rather a random thought, the Trigger can be lessened. For example, you may hear a text message come into a phone and immediately remember something about discovery of the Affair. At that moment, please remind yourself out loud or silently that you are in a safe place, that you have choices and one of them is to look at the phone to eliminate your anxiety or to walk away. Whatever you decide to do is exactly what you need to do at the moment. As each Trigger occurs, take a moment to assess your anxiety level and "rewrite" the narrative in your brain. I want to reassure you that while it may seem impossible to happen, you will get through the moment. Our thoughts are powerful, including soothing, comforting thoughts.

The triggers can be too numerous to expand on completely, but here are a few:

- Was the cell phone the connection to the Affair person? The phone must become available to the Betrayed person. Allow access to your phone whenever needed by your loved one. Changing your number is an option.

- Did this happen at work? The Betrayer may have to find another job.

- Did you discover the affair through a bank statement or a receipt?

- Was it a friend of the family? You may have to move.

- Was it your best friend? This requires an extremely difficult conversation about continuing or ending the friendship.

- Was it your partner's best friend's spouse?

- Was it a one-night stand? Depending on where this happened, routes may have to change to get to destinations.

- Did the person bring the Affair person into the house? You may have to sell your house.

- Did you meet at certain places and times?

- Was connection made through email? You may have to create new emails.

- Does the Affair person live close by? Again, you may have to move.

- Did you meet the person at the gym or other social event? You may have to switch gyms or social events.

- Did you meet the person at school? Grocery store? While shopping?

- Did the Affair take place during a holiday or a special time period?

- Did the Affair last years?

- Were there gifts exchanged?

- Was the Affair person met at Church? You may have to go to another

  Church.

- Watching a favorite TV show or a movie can also trigger feelings about the Affair. I suggest to my couples to monitor the subject matter of the program or movie and if it contains any type of relationship problems, perhaps switch to more lighthearted or religious based programs.

- Were you secure in the absolute belief that your relationship was solid, and your partner was happy? This will be a trigger as well. How can trust and security be felt again if your relationship was solid?

As you can see, there are numerous triggers that can set your loved one's hurt response to happen repeatedly. There must be honest conversations about how to manage these triggers and how to reframe or eliminate any if possible.

I will give a list of ways to cope with triggers at the end of the book.

I ask the person Betrayed to try not to scorch the earth with their anger and rage.   I understand you want to, and I understand you need to release all the fire inside of you, but I'm going to ask you to not do that. This kind of pain and anger is like cancer, and it will grow and consume all parts of you if you allow it to continue.

But then what can you do?

You can express to your partner how incredibly hurt, angry, humiliated, embarrassed and rageful you feel. Use very descriptive words about exactly how you feel. Your world just fell apart, and you are most likely unsure about anything other than expressing your anger, which now is most important.

I would encourage that expressions of your intense hurt be done in a way that deeply expresses how different you feel now…. It's different, I understand. Sit with it, close your eyes, and scan your entire body from head to toe, and especially your heart, and then write down what that feels like. For some, it is that the body itself is hollow and it feels like it will never be whole again. For others, it's a burning explosion that just cannot be put out. For some, there is nothing, a vast emptiness that feels unexplainable. There is so much pain that the only way to get through the moment is to feel nothing. I understand. Whatever you are feeling, allow those feelings to happen and be acknowledged through the verbal word or through writing. The feelings will be intense, but you will get to the other side….it just takes time.

Journaling and Why Do It.

I do encourage journaling about your day-to-day feelings and experiences. I do this for two reasons:

First, it is a way to release feelings in a purely safe way. As you write down thoughts and feelings of what you are going through, you may experience a lessening of the trauma. You may also learn so much about yourself – your resolve to go forward and overcome even this most challenging time in your life. If you experience no changes -- keep writing – you will get to the place where you can actually feel the difference.

Second, it is a way to look back on your journey and see how far – or not – you have come. You can celebrate your recovery and if you are stuck, perhaps the journaling will uncover how you became stuck and give insights about how to unentangle yourself from this place of "stuckness" and understand what you need to do to go forward.

What You Need to Feel Emotionally Safe Again.

Emotional safety is gone, guarantees of stability are gone, trust is gone, your future as you knew it is gone, so how can you recapture these fundamental foundations in your relationship and your life.

You can explain to your partner what you need to feel "safe" again.

If you are not sure what that would be, take time to reflect.

Remember…. trust cannot be restored until a sense of safety is restored.

Building trust is the primary steppingstone now in healing.

You may need to have access to all the accounts, passwords, and anything else that was associated with the Affair. Some of my clients have even put a GPS on the Betrayer's car. It seems the one place where an Affair is first discovered is through text messages. If you need to monitor the phone for a while, then that is okay.

You may want to hear the termination of the Affair firsthand, and you may want the Affair person to know you are listening to the end of the Affair. Whatever you need to feel safe, I encourage you to express it now. It will be hard, and it may seem impossible to do -- but try.

Do You Need to be a Private Investigator?

Do you need every single detail of the Affair? I always counsel my clients that it is best not to know every single detail because your memory will take an exceptionally long time to forget it. You will begin to cross reference details with times you were told lies. You will replay scenarios of when the person was late or did not come home at all. For some, enormous amounts of time and even joyful moments with the Betrayer will be tainted because of the length of the Affair. Those times will be seen as insincere and false…. but let me remind you, if you did have a good time, if you did laugh and feel love, then please keep that feeling and memory. Please do not erase your history…. Those moments are yours to keep. For some, that time will forever be thought of as a time of destruction…. even if there were moments during this period where you had a good time. Please don't erase or rewrite all your good memories which only erase parts of your life. The Affair will not win this battle of erasing your history. Keep what you like and toss the rest. Take back your life and your own unique history and vow to make new memories and joyful moments in your life.

I have not had a client who wants to be a private investigator forever in their relationship. So, my advice is to try to make this short lived in your life. If you cannot trust your partner as time goes on and you are trying everything you can to reconnect and rebuild, you may need to ask yourself, will you ever? Only you

will be able to answer this question honestly.

Managing The Torrent of Emotions. There is a choice for your

emotions to run you or for you to acknowledge your emotions, but you

decide not to let them run your life. Allow all that you need to feel be

felt.

It will not destroy you even though now it might seem that way.

Also, allow yourself the courage to harness those moments when you

want to strike out. It doesn't help in the long run to verbally annihilate

the Betrayer. On a daily basis, with 10 being the worst, try to give

yourself a score on the emotional distress you are under. When you go

below the highest number on one day, but the next day is worse try to

remember what you did that was different to change the distress score.

Maybe it was what the Betrayer did that helped. Whatever that is,

write it down, memorize it and try to duplicate those days that

decrease your stress levels.

Demonizing the Betrayer. The Betrayer is not evil…. It is

important to remember the Betrayer deserves the chance to restore

their own sense of self-worth. The Betrayer made an incredibly

stupid, selfish, and terrible mistake, but the Betrayer (at least I hope) is

not evil. You have the power to show mercy…. if you feel you can. If

not, I understand. But remember to hang on to this bitterness will only

keep you in a prison of emotional pain.   It will consume your every

waking hour and limit your ability to find joy in anything you do.

You have the power and strength to open the door to your emotional

prison and step outside.   You can do this.

   You Don't Have to Forgive. I know many will tell you that

"forgiveness" is the only way to heal completely but sometimes there

are just things that are unforgiveable.

   Let's take a moment and look at what forgiveness is:

Forgiveness is not given to the person who has hurt you because they

deserve it. Rather forgiveness is given because YOU deserve it. You

deserve to be free of the person's incredibly self-centered act so the deep, gut-wrenching pain that has highjacked your body and mind can be released.

Forgiveness also does not mean you will forget what happened – you will not. You may ask if not forgiveness to free you from this emotional prison, then what can you do?

One option that I offer my clients is that you can show *mercy* for a person who is flawed as a human being It may be a way that you can move past the bitterness and rage to a place that feels better inside you. By showing mercy, you are also giving yourself mercy and tenderness. These are behaviors that you most certainly deserve.

Perhaps you have the belief system that if you "forgive" or show "mercy", then who will be the keeper of the history of the terrible thing that has happened to you. After all, if you forgive or even show mercy, you may believe you are letting go, erasing or forgetting what happened to you. Who will advocate for you if not yourself Who will voice how horrible this was to you if not yourself. I can only say to you please don't stay in this prison of knowledge of the Affair. It is a fact. The facts will never change, but your life, your future and your peace of heart and mind can change, and I encourage you to allow that to happen whether you stay or leave.

Many times, the person who has been Betrayed takes on the role of a "therapist" for the person who has caused the traumatic event. I can understand slipping into this role because you may still be gathering facts about how this happened, but please don't do this. This person's emotional distress need not be placed upon you   Let that person seek their own therapist to alleviate you from taking on yet another burden from the Affair.

Acceptance. If forgiveness is not an option and showing mercy is a long way in the future, then perhaps you can just accept this is where you are now. Acceptance is not approval; you do not approve of the choices in behavior that have caused you so much pain, but you accept this is the reality of your situation now. Now you have gained back a little of your control of your life and that will be so beneficial as you go through this healing process.

Free Yourself of Guilt. I've had far too many people who have been

Betrayed question how on earth they missed the clues, missed what was going on, and it makes them feel like a failure.

Free your mind of any feelings of failure, guilt or shame. You did nothing wrong. I suggest you make a list of all that you have achieved in the relationship and all the ways you helped create an environment of loyalty, strength, and cherished love.

You were not a fool because it takes a lot of wisdom and strength to develop an environment with an atmosphere of complete trust and safety. Please don't let this moment in your life change your belief in these values you hold dear to your heart.

However, the nagging thoughts do creep up…. How did I miss the signs? Let me share with you some possible reasons:

- You missed the signs because there was assurance in the relationship that this would not happen.

- You missed the signs because the Betrayer was a good manipulator. A Betrayer wears many "masks"? You only saw the agreeable mask.

- You missed the signs because maybe you have been sick, and your sickness has depleted your energy to ask questions.

- You missed the signs because you were tired and exhausted from all that was required of you daily.

- You missed the signs because your family needed you on a daily basis. Perhaps your children or a family member was going through a particularly tough time.

- You missed the signs because there just weren't any.

- You missed the signs because it was easier to deny anything was happening. After all, most days were filled with behaviors of love toward you.

Most important is that You need not feel any guilt….ever. You did nothing to cause the person's decision to betray you.

  There must be an

understanding that: All communication between you and your

Betrayer needs to include transparency and genuine understanding

about the facts being presented. There must be attentive listening

evidenced by you from your Betrayer when you are discussing your

deep hurt and shock. The person who Betrayed does not have to "fix"

anything at this point, but rather, I encourage that while you are

showing remorse and empathy toward the person who has been hurt,

reframe from trying to "fix" the emotional intensity. The Betrayed

person needs to unload the emotional turmoil without anyone trying to

fix the moment. Listening is the best tool and "fixing" will come later,

but not in the beginning stage of recovery. Listen with your Heart.

In order to communicate with each other to achieve the best

possible outcome:

- The Betrayer needs to listen with intent which will encourage follow-up questions.

- There are no interruptions when you both are speaking.

- There is a softness in the Betrayer's eyes because the hurt is so evident.

- There are no distractions (no cell phones, no TV),
- There is respect for what the Betrayed person is going through and will go through for some time and most of all,

- There is a commitment to be patient, to be empathetic and to understand not just what the Betrayed person has gone through, but also what you went through to make the decision to cheat.

Changes in Behaviors and Attitudes. There must be observable changes in behavior and attitudes. In other words, if your relationship operates the same as it did when the Affair occurred, how will you ever have any assurance that it will not happen again? How will you know it is getting off track again?

Some clients have developed a "date night" that cannot be changed. Others have asked for more patience and understanding. "Do not interrupt me when I'm talking" – that is one I hear a lot. If you tell me you are coming home at a certain hour, then I expect you will do that, and if you can't, you will notify me by phone call or text.

One of the most important discussions will center around what the thought process of the Betrayer was to cross the line into infidelity.   This understanding by the Betrayer which must be concisely communicated to the Betrayed person will speed up the process of healing enormously. The Betrayer's thought process to come to the conclusion to be unfaithful is important for both of you. How will absolute certainty that this will not occur again be trusted if there is not an understanding of how it happened in the first place.

Reconnecting With Betrayer. You may feel a desperate need to reconnect with your Betrayer through physical intimacy. This is understandable, but in my practice, I've learned from my clients it does not take away the hurt and it does not take away the narrative playing in your mind. It only causes more emotional confusion.

Give yourself time to mourn the loss of the intimacy and innocence

you once had. I encourage my couples to build on personal

intimacy, sharing intimate knowledge that the other person never

knew. Sharing dreams about what could be the future. Sharing

worries as well as successes This is a time to bond in a more

personally intimate way. Sexual intimacy combined with a greater

depth of personal intimacy creates a stronger and more meaningful

bond.

Suggestions of Ways to Express Your Feelings. If you find it

hard to express how you are feeling and your deep wounds, you

may want to:

- Write a letter explaining how you see yourself, the

  relationship, and the future so differently.

- Where there was assurance of safety, now there is doubt.

  Express your doubt with an expression of confusion and

  uncertainty.

- Watch a movie together that explains how you feel better than you can.

- Where there was self-confidence, now there is diminished self-esteem. Maybe you don't feel attractive or desirable anymore. Remind yourself you are worthy of respect, fidelity, and honesty. You did nothing wrong. Also, remind the Betrayer that in one moment, the feelings of competence, assurance and self-esteem were suddenly stripped away, and it feels ______________ (what?)

- Where there were plans for the future, now all of that is on hold. Express your feelings of a future that seems nonexistent now; perhaps, there is actually no picture of it in your conscious awareness anymore . However, remember while the relationship future is foggy, your future can be yours…determine to make your future what you want or need it to be.

- Where there was blind trust, now there is only doubt and worry. Doubt and worry are evil twins. Replace these with the hope and ultimate knowledge you will get through this, and you will have trust in your life again – whether it is with your present person or someone else. You will even have trust in the world around you and have faith that a better future is available to you.

Belief System on Cheating. Many people who have been Betrayed had a long-standing belief about someone cheating on them ….have you said "If this ever happens to me, I'm out of here. I will not tolerate it" and "once a cheater, always a cheater." Or … "I can't believe my friend stayed. That person is so weak and I'm never going to be weak… It is humiliating and embarrassing seeing someone give in to forgiving a cheater".

I've heard all of these statements and more….so give yourself whatever time you need to wrap your head around this new "belief system" you are deciding for yourself. You may have to change your long-standing belief in staying or not and that is going to be exceedingly difficult, even agonizing. After all, if you change your belief system, then who are you? I have heard this said: "Are you telling me I need to change the core of who I am because of the person who Betrayed me" It is not the "core" of you that needs to change it may be your belief system about infidelity. As we evolve in this world, many times the belief system about certain subjects, people, or events changes. If you decide to stay in the relationship, you will need to "reframe" this belief system to one that fits who you are now.

Remember why you are changing your belief system … maybe your belief system was formed as a child, and you have more wisdom and maturity now or maybe it was formed from a prior relationship that had the same result as you are going through now. Whatever the case, honor your belief system first, and then decide whether you want to change it or keep it. No judgments – there is no right or wrong here.

I also am wondering whether in your life you have had to change your beliefs on other subjects, and it turned out (I hope) ok. That can be a guideline for you to have "hope" this too will turn out ok. If the answer is "no it didn't turn out ok", then it will be even harder to wrap your head around doing this. Give yourself time to really process this, write about it and allow whatever decision you need to make to be yours to honor and accept as your truth.

If you do decide to rephrase (not change completely) your belief about this particular subject, you will need to depend on your wisdom and strength to accept this must be done to save your relationship and your family.

The Partner Who Betrayed

You will have much of the responsibility for putting this relationship back together. There are certain fundamental behaviors and attitudes that must be used at this point.

Feeling Remorse Is Essential. If you don't feel remorse, then we have a bigger problem, don't we? Perhaps there are traumas in your life that have been unresolved that prevent you from this feeling…there is no judgment; just wondering. If that is the case, I recommend you seek therapy to process the traumas…. There is nothing more heartbreaking to me than to see one of my clients suffer deeply from severe traumas in their life and the person has not processed all those feelings to find peace. Because these trauma patterns have not been processed, your loved one becomes the person who must endure the consequence of unresolved trauma. It is my firm belief that we can never change events, but there is always hope that the feelings and the behaviors resulting from the traumatic events can be changed. I have seen it

happen….and it always brings me to tears.

As defined in the Oxford Learners Dictionary Remorse is:

"The feeling of being extremely sorry for something wrong or bad that you have done" (:remorse noun - Definition, pictures, pronunciation and usage notes | Oxford Advanced Learner's Dictionary at OxfordLearnersDictionaries.com)

To help you understand on a deeper level what Remorse looks like and how to express remorse in a meaningful and heartfelt way, the following is offered as suggestions:

The following behaviors and actions can show remorse. These are taken from a Google Search found on The Vessel *(powerful ways to show remorse without saying a word (thevessel.io)*

"1) Actions of empathy and understanding.
Showing empathy doesn't mean just saying "I understand you're hurt".

It's about truly putting yourself in the other person's shoes and feeling their pain.

Silently demonstrating understanding can be as simple as giving the person space when they need it, or being there for them when they're ready to talk.

It's about respecting their feelings and their process of dealing with the situation.

And remember, it's not about finding solutions or fixing things.

This is about showing that you acknowledge their hurt and that you are there with them in this challenging time."

2) The power of body language

Here's something we often overlook: our non-verbal cues.

Body language is a powerful communication tool that can express more than words ever could.

It's like a silent language that conveys our inner feelings and intent.

Now, you might be wondering how this ties in with expressing remorse. Well, think about it.

A genuine look of regret, a gentle touch on the shoulder, or even maintaining eye contact when the other person is speaking – these are all non-verbal cues that can express a sense of remorse and regret.

But here's the catch.

It has to be genuine.

People can usually tell when body language is forced or insincere. So, when you're using body language to express remorse, ensure it truly mirrors your feelings.

3) Embracing vulnerability

Following up on body language, there's another aspect of nonverbal communication that plays a crucial role in expressing remorse – vulnerability,

Here's why.

When we let our guard down, it shows the other person that we're being genuine.

It displays a level of trust and openness that words often fail to convey.

Allowing yourself to be seen in a vulnerable state, whether it's through tears, or simply an open, authentic expression of regret, speaks volumes about your remorse.

It's less about exposing your weaknesses and more about showing your genuine regret and willingness to mend things.

. . .

4) **Active Listening** is more than just hearing the words the other person is saying. It's about fully focusing on them, showing empathy, and understanding their perspective. you're trying to express remorse, try switching off your defensive mode for a bit, sit back, and just listen.

You'd be surprised how much this simple act can convey your genuine regret and desire to make amends.

5) Consistency is key

Consistency in showing remorse isn't about repeating "I'm sorry" like a broken record.

. . . true remorse is shown not in grand gestures or eloquent words, but in consistent actions over time."

Don't be defensive. Accept responsibility. Over and over and over again, you must express in words and actions how sorry you are. You must admit your mistakes and ask for mercy. You may not get it right away but genuine, heart-felt remorse is deeply needed.

Don't make excuses. You have hurt your loved one to the core; to make excuses now would only cause the hurt to increase and it would be mean and cruel to cause more hurt to your Betrayed partner. Accept blame and responsibility every single day until all has been resolved and processed.

Tact and gentleness will be important. Please do not start a sentence with "well, you……" This will only lead to a defensive response and then another defensive response from you. I understand that there are issues in the relationship…. if there weren't any…. this would not have happened. However, now is not the time to bring up every unresolved conflict…. let's just stick to resolving the Affair and finding a way forward.

Transparency is not just important….it is the only thing in the beginning that can assure recovery. There is no reason to hide anything anymore because omission can also be described as "lying by omission". Please don't do that.   Your relationship is shattered into pieces. Holding back on any information about the Affair now is futile. If a question is asked, please answer it truthfully. Should you not, and later on your partner finds out there is yet more information, trust and safety are once again destroyed, and there is a high likelihood that will be the end of your relationship.

  Do not, and I will repeat, do not put blame on the relationship or the person who has been Betrayed. There is only one person who consciously decided to cross the line into infidelity…. And that is the person who has committed the Affair. I understand the relationship was most likely in trouble, and I understand there are circumstances that need to be addressed…. but not now. After all, it was a conscious decision that was made and one that needs to be understood by you. In other words, how did you come to the conclusion that this was okay to do?   What were the pros and cons? Did you consider the fantasy could never compete with reality? Did you consider the tsunami of hurt and pain that would follow after discovery of the Affair?

Did you realize how much it would hurt your family, your friends, your co-workers, your church affiliations (if you have some), and your own perspective about who you really are? It's just as hard for the

Betrayer to accept the truth about the infidelity that caused so much pain.

After all, your reputation is at stake here, and you may have believed you

would never make this decision in your relationship.

Perhaps it was purely an emotional decision….and then the next

question must be about your innate behavior to follow a purely emotional

response. Has this been a problem in the past? Have you found yourself

in compromising situations based on your response to your intense

emotions?

Was drinking or any type of prescription or other drug involved?

There are numerous hidden reasons for the decision to cheat. It is up to

the Betrayer to search inside and come up with the reasons. How can

your loved one ever trust you again if you are not able to articulate why

you choose to do this. If there is no roadmap to "infidelity" that you can

lay out for your hurt loved one, how on earth is that person going to know

if all is going well or not. Can you be trusted? Is this a once in a lifetime

mistake? Were all the times spent with your loved one expressing love

and devotion all a lie? Reflect on what was really going on with you, and find the answers that your loved one deserves to hear that are authentic and true. How will you forever be faithful?

Alcohol and/or Drug Problems. Is there an issue with alcohol or drug abuse? If there is, the first step for recovery for you is to seek help with your addiction. You cannot be truly transparent if this is kept a secret.

Journal. As I stated before, journaling is an effective way to reflect on your decision-making process. It is also a time to understand what you are feeling about what has happened. Spend some time alone and determine in your heart what happened that caused you….not your partner or the relationship….to cross the line into infidelity. Journaling will be your own private journey to healing.

Be Patient. Just because you are changing behaviors and trying to build trust, don't expect that your loved one will accept these new behaviors as evidence that you have changed. Give it time and keep making the changes. See this time as building a "new normal" not only for yourself but for your relationship. Try not to feel defeated when for

the thousandth time you have stated you are sorry and the response of

not believing you remains unchanged. It takes a while for "defensive

arguments" from your partner not to be part of any conversation. I

understand it's hard to hear over and over again the fact that you are a

Betrayer. With time and a dedicated resolve to change and understand,

this will become easier, and the defensive arguments will lessen.

Personal Therapy Helps. Please get your own individual

therapy. Most people would never guess that they would cheat, but here

it is. You may feel lower than low or a failure in so many ways. You are

not. You have made a terrible selfish mistake and one that you have now

accepted responsibility for. Allow yourself the opportunity to gain more

information about who you are by engaging in therapy. That could be

through your Church or a professional therapist, but please consider it.

Keep It Honest. Do not share with your loved one that you were

going to end it anyway before it was found out. That statement will not be believed. It is "crazy making" to your loved one and it is not a realistic fact. Please don't encourage the person to believe something they know is just not true. You got caught; that is the fact. If you were going to end it, you wouldn't be where you are right now. Be honest.

You may have thought I can't do this anymore, this is wrong, I must end this, but the bottom line is that you did not.

The Past Is Still the Present Until It's Not. I have heard the words, why can't we move forward? You keep bringing up the same thing every day. I feel we are always going to the past and never going forward". There is really a simple reason for this – because the past is still in the present. Unless new behaviors, new attitudes, new learnings about your partner and new belief systems are established and play out every single day, the past will remain in the present. That is why I strongly encourage my couples to develop new rituals in the relationship, new norms, whatever you want to call it and keep it sacred to your everyday activities. The standard is it takes 30 days to create a new behavior and for an Affair, it takes longer than that.

II THE ACUTE STAGE – AND BEYOND

Once there is a lessening of anxiety, depression and outright rage, the next phase to recovery begins. I want to emphasize do not rush The Critical Stage because it is in that stage that a new foundation of trust and safety to your relationship is starting to be formed, and a new future is beginning to take shape. A "new normal" starts to emerge and there is a softening of the heart. I didn't say the heart melted, only a softening.

Continue Working on What you Have Learned

At this stage in recovery, there may be more questions than answers. Hopefully, time has passed, and you both have been working on being transparent, offering remorse and expressing empathy, but you may feel incredibly stuck. For instance:

You may state we keep trying and trying and doing what is laid out in this book, but I'm not feeling we are getting anywhere. I do understand this. Most people are used to quick fixes, but that won't happen with an

Affair. I continue to encourage my couples to keep doing what is

working. Remember repetition of behaviors that are working can bring a

sense of newness and a better understanding of what works for you both.

This is a marathon relationship race not a sprint. In order to have

assurance that the "new" relationship is worth all this work and time,

we need to accept that the time spent in doing these repair efforts will

be worth it

III HEALING AND RECOVERY

Healing and Recovery are strange concepts in themselves. How does a person know when healing is occurring from an Affair. After all, it is not like a flesh wound that you can see heal. It is inside and in all parts of your body and your mind…from the feelings of light headedness to your knees buckling, to your feet not wanting to walk forward. Your body suffers all kinds of emotional attacks from discovering an Affair.

So, what are the guidelines and is it linear or huge boulders to overcome? I can assure you it is not linear – there will be periods of time when you can feel a sense of peace of heart and see the healing taking place, and then, without any reason, another setback occurs. Just remember even with a setback, you have come a long way from ground zero.

Recovery is another concept that is hard to determine, but if you can give your relationship some goals or guidelines to "measure" recovery, then there is the possibility that you will be able to witness the recovery taking place.

The question I am asked the most is "Will I ever not think about this and feel horrible about this Affair?" I have no actual answer to this other than if you choose to keep the Affair alive by forever remembering the events, talking about the events, revisiting those places where the Affair occurred or even making yourself remember the anniversary dates for the Affair, you will forever live in the past without giving present day a chance.

Let me share a story. I had a woman come to see me and she was depressed and heartbroken that her husband had Betrayed her. She did get a divorce, but she was still suffering, and I could see it in her body, which resembled someone carrying the emotional weight of the world on their shoulders, and her eyes – the window to the soul – showed so clearly she was in agony.   So, I asked her when did this happen, and she replied, "30 years ago!". To say I was sad for her is an understatement. Much of her life had been spent discussing and reminiscing about how horrible her husband had treated her and how humiliated and broken she had become. In fact, only a few years ago she passed away still clinging to the victimization she suffered by the Affair in her past. Please don't let this be you.

How long has it been from the beginning knowledge of the Affair? As I explained before, research shows it takes an average of 2 years to fully recover. Where do you think your relationship is right now? If you are still in the beginning stages of recovery, please do not feel defeated – there is no linear line of recovery, much like grief. It takes whatever time is needed for your unique relationship to realign to a relationship that is at peace.

Gifts of Kindness

This concept is for both of you. Gifts of Kindness are just that …a daily reminder of how lucky and fortunate you are on this day to be rebuilding the relationship. Some examples include:

- Let your partner know how incredibly and genuinely grateful you are that the agreement was made to stay together.

- Remind your partner that for the rest of your life you want to live up to and humbly honor their "leap of faith" in you.

- Let your partner know how beautiful, handsome, thankful, unselfish, kind and incredibly strong of them to allow this rebuilding to take place.

- Remind them you will never forget their generosity and remind yourself to live up to this declaration – even in those most difficult times.

- Spontaneously do something that they did not ask you to do but you know it needs to be done.

- Thank them over and over again for this opportunity.

- Tell them how important they are in your life and how incredibly stupid you were to do what you did.

- Thank your partner for being patient with you.

- Again, say you are sorry for the thousandth time.

- Let them know you do not think of them as a horrible person.

- Let them know through words and actions that your decision is not a reflection of anything wrong with them. The choice was yours and you accept all consequences.

- Let them know your choice to stay and rebuild the relationship is not from a sense of obligation to the Betrayed partner and family, but to the unwavering fact that your love is deeper now than ever before.

These are only a small number of suggestions, but look around, and whatever you feel you need to do to give a "Gift of Kindness" then do that.

The Journey of Healing is for Both Partners

Healing from an Affair cannot be done on an "island" of selfpreservation. If you decide to stay together to work on rebuilding the relationship, you cannot recover and heal alone. It will take both of you to rebuild the relationship and offer insightful and meaningful conversations about what you are both feeling, what you both want for the future, what you are willing to accept and what you are adamant that you cannot accept.

For the Betrayed partner, the person who can help you heal this terrible hurt is the person who has caused it. It seems inconceivable that the person who Betrayed you would be the one person to ask for help in developing trust and safety once again, but if you are going to stay, it is necessary.

However, you will not use "blind trust" at this point. Instead, you will insist upon developing new norms, new rituals, and new behaviors to begin to develop "trust" in the relationship. A person can say whatever they want – they can express remorse and extreme sorrow for what you have been put through – but consistent, long-term change in behaviors will win the day of rebuilding trust and safety.

What I have witnessed is that in the beginning all parties are willing to do whatever is needed to bring about a sense of peace and calm in the relationship. However, two, three or four months down the road and suddenly, frustration sets in and remarks like "aren't we over this yet" or "how long before we don't talk about this daily", or "it doesn't matter what I do, you will never trust me again" begin to emerge.

Should you encounter any statements like this, or you feel a sense of "heaviness" because it's never "over," please remember the world changed the day the Affair was discovered, and it takes whatever length of time necessary to rebuild a new "relationship world".

You both have decided to stay together and work toward a "new relationship" and I give you both a lot of credit for this decision. But the work is ongoing……until it's not anymore. You will know when it's better because you may have an entire day where you don't feel weighted down, you feel lighter, more optimistic and more balanced; like your world is realigning itself to a new normal and one you can trust.   As you go through the hours and days of learning about the Affair, you each will need to allow the relationship to "rise from the ashes." If you cannot do this, it doesn't sound the alarm that it can't heal, but it does mean it will take longer.

It is the expression of remorse that allows safety to be rebuilt and healing and recovery to begin. Some people have a tough time allowing remorse to be present in the healing process for any length of time. It's okay to display deep remorse for a while, but then it becomes difficult to tolerate showing this feeling anymore. I can understand that the person who has caused the Affair does not want to experience the shame and guilt to wash over them once more, but it is necessary. Deep remorse signals to the person Betrayed that because the person feels the same kind of hurt the Betrayed person is feeling that it will not happen again. I've been asked "How long do I have to say I'm sorry? My response is always the same – "Until the person you Betrayed tells you it's enough." It is believed that if the person has said "I'm sorry" and that "it will never happen again" all should be well – but that kind of thinking is just not the case.

Now is the time to take what you have learned and put that into practice in your relationship with new rituals and norms, such as:

- What is your nighttime ritual? Do you say goodnight? Do you both go to bed at the same time? Do you cuddle? I once had a couple who watched TV in separate rooms and then went to bed without ever saying goodnight or acknowledging to the other the day was over. This makes for a lot of loneliness and leads to some bad decisions.

- Do you have a date night? I have suggested to my clients that they get a babysitter (if you have children) and set up a weekly time the babysitter is to be at your house. Then every week go do something during the time you have a sitter. If you don't have children, then make the most of this cherished time you both have decided is your "special time together."

- My other suggestion for my couples is to create a "fun jar". Get a jar of any kind and when you read something or you know something you would like to do, write it down, fold it up and put it in the jar. Then, weekly, or monthly, take turns and close your eyes and take one suggestion out of the jar. The goal is that you both will be willing to do what is written down (within reason of course). For instance, for me and my husband, anything dealing with cars he will want to do, and I agree to do that, as he agrees

  to go to museums, plays and lectures that I might like. This is an opportunity to not only begin the practice of a new ritual, but also perhaps to get to know each other on a deeper level.

- Another ritual I suggest is to create a "Mantra of this House" board to be framed and put on the wall. For example, this House encourages open and honest communication without judgment; this House uses "I'm sorry" and "Thank you" as expressions of genuine regard to others, "This House helps one another to become the person they want to be". As you can see, there can be a lot of Mantras that can be included. Make whatever is right for your House, and if you have children, include their suggestions as well.

- How do we greet each other in the morning and at the end of the day? Do you give each other a kiss, a hug, a treat? Whatever it is, make sure that is a ritual that lasts.

- How do you celebrate anniversaries, birthdays, holidays, and special events? Can you change anything from the past to make these milestones in your relationship more meaningful?

- Do you attend Church? Are you volunteering? Are these responsibilities important to you? If so, what rituals can you include to make these behaviors important?

- How do you disagree? What is your signal to the other for a "time out". And how do you support a time-out? I encourage my couples to try to resolve issues before bedtime, but if that can't be done then "symbolically" put the issue in a box with

the promise it will be discussed and figured out the next day.
Please don't let unresolved issues linger for too long. It only
encourages more avoidance of discussing the issue. And
remember, sometimes there is no "win/win"; sometimes there is
only "accept/accept".

- Share with each other something learned that day either about
themselves, the world in general and/or about the other person.

- Celebrate being together. How will you celebrate your success
in getting through this tough time?

- Will you renew your vows of the relationship? I have had
several couples write down the many steps taken to healing and
recovery, and then, when you are both at a place where it is a
new beginning, ceremoniously tear up the paper. Then they
write down the new vows of the relationship and keep it to
review yearly as a reminder of their commitment to each other.

- How do you let the other person know how important they are
in your life? Make it a point to do so daily.

As always, these are suggestions. I'm sure you can come up with a lot more for your relationship.

Define What the Consequences Will be If an Affair Happens Again

I can almost hear you say: There will be no discussion. The Relationship will be over for good – period the end!

But let's say your partner runs late one too many times or misses an important event. What if someone is flirting with your partner? What happens if your partner seems tired of working on the relationship or work takes your partner away a lot?

These are areas of a relationship that don't require rules in the beginning but when an Affair occurs, new standards for the relationship need to be voiced and then a commitment made to abide by them.

There is a need for each partner to explain how fidelity and infidelity will be defined and what will be the consequences. Be specific as you can.

You can write columns on a sheet of paper with the Words "What is Acceptable in our Relationship to Ensure Fidelity" and then "What is Unacceptable in our Relationship to Ensure Fidelity".

Infidelity can come in many disguises so take a moment and determine what an act of Infidelity looks like, sounds like or feels like. What is the line you both will not cross?   For each couple, the terms will be different.

You don't want to make the relationship so restrictive you can't enjoy life in general, so be flexible and open to compromise.

How to Stand Together as One

What does that mean? It means the two of you will begin to create a mutual narrative about the relationship and what caused the damage. You both have different perspectives about the Affair and now is the moment to bring both perspectives into one – it means combining what is "acceptable" from both perspectives and what is "not acceptable" and agreeing as a couple that this new narrative will be founded on mutual understanding and respect for each other's perspective. One person may state "I cannot at this time forgive the Affair, but I'm willing to allow and acknowledge new behaviors". Another approach may be "I don't understand your perspective, but I appreciate your sharing it with me." "I can only imagine how hard this is for you, and I appreciate your giving us an opportunity to rebuild our relationship. How can I make it easier for you". "What can I do to make our life better – what did I do before you did not like and how can I change it". Look at the suggested examples, notice "I" statements are used exclusively. The purpose and goal will be to begin meaningful and stress-reducing conversations between the two of you. It's not easy, but with practice, it can become a "new normal".

Take time each day to start preparing your new narrative. This also gives you both an opportunity to discuss something so traumatic in a more structured way.

As you both show to the world that you are coming together once again, your family and friends will have no choice but to respond with kindness to your courage and strength.   It does not mean that work on the relationship stops – but it allows you to show others that healing is happening, and recovery is possible.

How to Develop a New Narrative About the Relationship

Let me first introduce a better way to communicate so that the conversation does not escalate into bedlam.   Some of these ways to communicate have been around for a long time, so you may know some of these suggestions already:

Begin your statements with "I".   If you begin with "you" then defensiveness will immediately emerge.   As an example: "I feel unsure about this exercise, but I'm willing to try". If you begin with you: "You caused this, you cheated, you are not a victim", you will only create the perfect situation to become defensive and a meaningful narrative cannot be accomplished. "

I'm always amazed when a critical "you" statement is made and then the other person gets defensive and the person who made the critical remark is surprised at the defensiveness. Of course, they will. That's why using "I"

statements as much as possible is so important. When I hear someone state

to the person being defensive "Don't take it so personal" I have to remind

them it is very personal when a person's character is attacked. The behavior

of the Affair is one thing…. but attacking the character of either person will

only lead to more unresolved conflict.

Use Active Listening. This means being completely engaged in

the conversation without forming in your mind your own counter opinion

or argument.   You may even summarize for your partner what you

heard and ask if what you are hearing is correct. If not, then ask for

further clarification. I have a quote I have put on my computer. It reads:

"God gave us two ears and one mouth so we can listen better". It's true.

Active listening is our most powerful recovery tool.

Be approachable. Bring your most open and emotionally reachable

self to this discussion. Before any conversation about the Affair, I advise

my clients to close their eyes, take some deep breaths and allow a sense of

calm to be felt within them.

Set aside all other forms of communication. Turn off everything else, including phones.

Make an Appointment. Make sure you "made an appointment" with each other for this discussion. This will avoid any interruptions and last minute "oh, I forgot I have to do this", or "I really only have a few minutes".

If you are religious, you may want to offer a prayer of guidance during these difficult conversations.

If you have children, make sure the children are occupied or out of the home while you discuss this new narrative.

Finding the Right Place to Discuss the Affair. You may also decide not to discuss things in the home at all but rather go to a park or a place that invites calm and peace for you both. Once I had a discussion like this in my car in the parking lot of my Church. I felt safe and peaceful there.

Time Limit. Give this discussion a time limit….30-60 minutes is enough.

Prepare Discussion Points. Write down before the discussion the main points you want to express.

What Triggers the Ending of the Discussion. Have some idea about when you have reached a stopping point and then stop and set up another appointment within the next week.

Ask as Many Questions as You Need to. Show curiosity about the other person. Ask questions – don't just answer questions.

What is the New Narrative. Both partners should have an opportunity to state what they consider the new narrative to be. If it is agreeable to you both, then accept this new narrative. This will not be the only time you create a new narrative. As time passes, I encourage my couples to meet again, or as many times as needed, to create an updated version of the new narrative.

REMEMBER – These discussions are to "learn" more about each other The reason we have conversations at all is to share ourselves on a deeper level. We may believe that we know everything there is to know about the other person, but in my experience, we do not.   Just the other day, my husband of over 20 years shared something with me I never

knew. I felt so surprised and yet so honored to know a new truth about

my husband.

IV. WHAT MADE THE RELATIONSHIP VULNERABLE

As your recovery and healing begin to take place and new ways of communicating are introduced as well as new norms and rituals, I encourage you both to look at the relationship with the critical eye to what happened that made the relationship vulnerable.

This is the hard part and the final part. You both are at a place to focus on the relationship completely and honestly. I understand we want to blame the other partner for the problems, but wouldn't it be better to see where the problems may have arisen and how to eliminate those problems.

So, do not fear this last part of healing. You've come a long way, and you will get through this Here are some examples of questions to answer yourself and your partner:

- How was fidelity defined in your relationship?

- Did you "fight fair" …in other words, did someone have to win the argument or was there room for compromise?

- Did arguments use what I call "verbal annihilation" to make a point? That's when words that belittle, demean and make others feel small are used ?

- Were there behaviors and verbal exchanges that felt threatening?

- How did you celebrate your relationship and each other?

- What was your communication like? As I tell my couples:

    You are always communicating even when you aren't speaking. There is a conversation style that is more damaging than others, and that is: **silent defiance**. It causes unspoken frustrations, anxiety and separateness from each other.

- Did you both agree on parenting (if you have children)?

- Did you both agree on in-law visits or stays?

- Were you walking on eggshells, even though there was a "front" that all was well?

- Did the relationship have a defined plan for how each person's profession would be honored?

- Did the relationship struggle with an addiction of one member of the family or several members?

- How was religion or "no religion" managed?

- Was higher education an issue?

- How were finances managed? Was one person in charge or both?

- Was the relationship transparent in its ability to discuss difficult issues?

- Did one partner want more sex than the other?

- Where you able to define the difference between "personal intimacy" and "sexual intimacy"?

- Did you rely on "blind trust" and the belief system nothing – especially cheating – would ever happen.

These, and many other areas of your relationship need to be explored, and questions answered honestly.

What I have found with most couples is that they mention they do

not have disagreements. It is my opinion that when there are no

disagreements there is not true authenticity or vulnerability and safety

in the relationship. We all have ways of irritating the other person in

our relationship. If there was no room for discussion of these

differences, or if the differences were discussed, and nothing changed,

then we need to ask the question and explore "why". Is it from the

dynamics of the relationship or past unresolved childhood issues or just

because there is so much going on in the relationship, you are too tired

to disagree, and it is easier to just "agree".

As a Gottman trained couples' therapist, I use the principles of John

and Julie Gottman in my therapy and will share with you here a handout I

give to my couples which summarizes what I consider to be the most

damaging communication patterns for a couple. It is called: "Harsh

Start-ups and The Four Foremen" and it clearly shows how toxic and

damaging communication patterns can destroy a relationship.   I hope it

will help you recognize when the relationship is in trouble. Please read this over without judgment, but wanting to have more knowledge about how to rebuild the relationship on solid principles and well-documented research.   I call this "When a Relationship Is in Trouble":

According to John and Julie Gottman (1999, 2015):

"HARSH STARTUP

The most obvious indicator that a discussion (and the relationship) is not going to go well is the way it begins. When a discussion leads off with criticism and/or sarcasm, a form of contempt — it has begun with a "harsh startup."

The research shows that if your discussion begins with a harsh startup, it will inevitably end on a negative note, even if there are a lot of attempts to "make nice" in between. Statistics tell the story: 96 percent of the time you can predict the outcome of a conversation based on the first three minutes of the fifteen-minute interaction!

A harsh startup simply dooms you to failure. So, if you begin a discussion that way, you might as well pull the plug, take a breather, and start over.

THE FOUR HORSEMEN

"A harsh startup sounds the warning bell that the couple may be having serious difficulty." As the discussion unfolds, negative interactions also unfold. Certain kinds of negativity, if allowed to run rampant, are so lethal to a relationship. These negative interactions are called the Four Horsemen of the Apocalypse. Usually these four horsemen clip-clop into the heart of a relationship in the following order: criticism, contempt, defensiveness, and stonewalling.

Horseman 1: Criticism. You will always have some complaints about the person you live with. But there's a world of difference between a complaint and a criticism.

A complaint only addresses the specific action at which your partner failed. A criticism is more global — it adds on some negative words about your mate's character or personality. A criticism implies something is wrong with the person not the behavior.

"I'm really angry that you didn't sweep the kitchen floor last night. We agreed that we'd take turns doing it" is a complaint — it focuses on a specific behavior.

"Why are you so forgetful? I hate having to always sweep the kitchen floor when it's your turn. You just don't care" is a criticism. Criticism throws in blame and general character assassination. To turn a complaint into a criticism, add the line: "What is wrong with you.

Usually, a harsh startup comes in the guise of criticism.

Complaint. There's no gas in the car. Why didn't you fill it up like you said you would?

. Why can't you ever remember anything? I told you a thousand times to fill up the tank, and you didn't. (Criticism. The implication is that it is all the other person's fault. Even if it is, blaming the other person will only make it worse.

The first horseman is very common in relationships. If you find that you and your partner are critical of each other, don't assume you're headed for divorce court. The problem with criticism is that when it becomes pervasive, it paves the way for the other, far deadlier horsemen.

Antidote for Criticism: Use Gentle Start-up. For instance, begin with "I" statements rather than "You" statements. A "you" statement starts out criticizing the person but an "I" statement comes from a place of respect but also a need to express frustration in a behavior.

Horseman 2: Contempt. Sarcasm and cynicism are types of

contempt. So are name-calling, eye-rolling, sneering, mockery, and hostile humor. In whatever form, contempt — the worst of the four horsemen — is poisonous to a relationship because it conveys disgust. It's virtually impossible to resolve a problem when your partner is getting the message you're disgusted with him or her. Inevitably, contempt leads to more conflict rather than to reconciliation.

Often a person's main purpose is to demean their partner. Couples who are contemptuous of each other are more likely to suffer from infectious illnesses (colds, flu, and so on) than other people.

Contempt is fueled by long-simmering negative thoughts about the partner. You're more likely to have such thoughts if your differences are not resolved. As disagreement persists, complaints turn into global criticisms, which produces more and more disgusted feelings and thoughts, and finally you are fed up with your partner, a change that will affect what you say when you argue.

Belligerence is just as deadly to a relationship. It is a form of aggressive anger because it contains a threat or provocation.

Antidote for Contempt: Build a Culture of Appreciation for each other.

Do you routinely express your gratefulness to each other? Do you find time to express thankfulness for your partner's patience, understanding and their own perspective? All of these are ways to increase your appreciation for each other.

Horseman 3: Defensiveness. When conversations become so negative, critical, and attacking, it should come as no surprise that you will defend yourself.

Although this is understandable, research shows that this approach rarely has the desired effect. The attacking partner does not back down or apologize. This is because defensiveness is really a way of blaming your partner.

You're saying, in effect, "The problem isn't me, it's you."

Defensiveness just escalates the conflict, which is why it's so deadly.

Criticism, Contempt, and Defensiveness don't always gallop into a home in strict order. They function more like a relay match — handing the baton off to each other repeatedly if the couple can't put a stop to it. The more defensive one becomes, the more the other attacks in response. Nothing gets resolved, thanks to the prevalence of criticism, contempt, and defensiveness.

Much of these exchanges are communicated subtly (and not so subtly) through body language and sounds.

Antidote for Defensiveness: Take Responsibility. Focus on what was going on and what your role was in causing the argument. Could be you were tired or physically not feeling well. Whatever you discover that may have led to the argument, express your responsibility.

Horseman 4: Stonewalling. In relationships where discussions begin with a harsh startup, where criticism and contempt lead to defensiveness, which leads to more contempt and more defensiveness, eventually one partner tunes out. So enters the fourth horseman.

Think of the partner who comes home from work, gets met with a barrage of criticism from their partner and hides . . . . . . The less responsive the partner is, the more yelling takes place. Eventually, the partner gets up and leaves the room. Rather than confronting their partner, the person disengages. By turning away, the partner has avoided a fight, but the partner is also avoiding the relationship. This becomes stonewalling.

A stonewaller doesn't give you (any) sort of casual feedback. They tend to look away or down without uttering a sound. The person will sit impassive and like a stone wall. The stonewaller acts as though they couldn't care less about what you're saying.

Stonewalling usually arrives later during a relationship than the other three horsemen. That's why it's less common among newlyweds than among couples who have been in a negative spiral for a while. It takes time for the negativity created by the first three horsemen to become overwhelming enough that stonewalling becomes an understandable "out."

: Use physiological soothing techniques.

Breathing deeply and releasing your breath slowly can immediately lower your heart rate. Stating to your partner the need for a calmer approach to the problem will give you a chance to express what is going on with you. If needed, tell your partner you need a break from the argument to allow yourself some time to regain your equilibrium."

I hope this brief summary of some of the Gottman communication principles offers insight….not blame….into how your relationship could have gotten off track

V COPING WITH TRIGGERS

One of the most damaging reoccurring problems I hear is that the Betrayed person is constantly triggered by events daily. I am going to recommend some coping strategies, but the best strategy is the one that works best for you:

There are many therapies available to reduce the tape player and movie screen running in your thoughts, but I do believe some have proven better than others.

Let me begin by stating my immediate coping strategy and that is I believe in divine help. As a Christian, I turn to my God to help me through the most difficult times and perhaps that is where you will get your most beneficial help. If you are not religious, there is no judgment here. Find whatever is stronger than you and then ask for help.

Here are some suggestions that my couples have shared with me that helped them:

The first one is Cognitive Behavior Therapy techniques, and you probably have heard of these. The most important is to remember

- What our thoughts are

- Determine what we are feeling.

- And then what we are feeling determines our response in behaviors.

As you can see, it all starts with our thoughts. Controlling our thoughts will be the first obstacle. But thoughts are random and unexpected, aren't they? So, I encourage my clients to "reframe" their thoughts as much as possible. For example, we may think "I was so stupid, He/She never loved me really, how humiliating, how embarrassing, I will never be the same again". These thoughts are destructive. They create a perspective and narrative about who you are that is just not accurate. By reframing and using more fact-based statements about your strength, courage, resilience, and just plain determination to change and go forward you can begin to change the negative narrative.

Here are some examples:

- "I did not see the facts because the manipulation was so good.

- It is true that many times I did feel loved and safe and that is

  a fact.

- My humiliation and embarrassment will only be responded to if I see myself as deserving of humiliation and embarrassment.

- I deserve respect and I will conduct myself with respect for myself.

- I will get over this and I will be different but also better.

- I will show myself mercy.

I hope you can see how changing even a few words we are repeating in our thoughts can change the whole way we think about events and ourselves.

The second coping skill I want to recommend is learn how to meditate. I also want to include in the idea of meditation the practice of prayer.

I am a certified Guided Imagery Therapist with many years of practice not only in my therapy practice but in hospitals working with cancer patients. Using meditation daily, practicing deep breathing exercises and allowing your mind to be free of all incoming thoughts allows the brain to go on what I call a "mental vacation". This slows down the destruction of the Affair by putting on hold all the stored-up rage and anger. I remind my clients the body does not know what it doesn't know. So, if is not given moments of relief from the affair, it cannot repair itself emotionally, physically and mentally.

The body will remember everything associated with the traumatic event, so even the time of day, a smell, a refreshing breeze, or a pleasant feeling will be stored in the body, and without notice, the body and mind will respond as though the discovery of the Affair is happening in real time. So, if the body remembers everything, then we need to change how the body responds, and the only way I know how to do that is to practice meditation or prayer – or both.   It will never erase the facts of the Affair, but it will give you a chance to calm your mind and the feelings around the

Affair. It then helps the brain begin a new and different thought pattern.

You can find guided meditations on the internet and at local bookstores. If you give yourself about 20 minutes a day to practice any type of meditation, I am hopeful you will find it will also change the trauma now playing in your thoughts and your anxiety will be reduced.

The third coping behavior that I have found strongly helps individuals is to discover the healing properties of being around nature. Go for walks, hikes, bike riding or any other activity that allows you the absolute freedom of enjoying nature and how it can "heal" you. If you only have 5 or 10 minutes to spare, it's a beginning and that is what we are looking for…. The beginning of a new behavior that will then become a lifelong behavior.

The fourth coping behavior that I can recommend is love yourself. There is nothing more healing and allows us to reframe our thoughts than to turn to ourselves and give ourselves love.   Whether that is a big hug, to giving ourselves permission to cry as much as we want, and allowing ourselves the empathy needed at this most difficult time – whatever is needed, give that to yourself.   We may not believe we are loved, but we can change that thought by loving who we are.

These are the only coping behaviors I'm going to share. I know it is a short list, but I believe that if you try to do any one of these consistently, you will find the constant tape playing over and over in your head will have no choice but to change its narrative and your stress level will be reduced.

VI FINAL OBSERVATIONS

This time in your life will be one of turmoil, confusion, dismay, unbelievable pain and eventually, peace, understanding and wisdom. I understand how hard the road is to get to healing and recovery because I have witnessed it through my clients, and I have gone through it myself.

I hope this book of suggestions and encouragements will help you as you courageously decide to go down the road to healing.

Lastly, I send you roses from my heart that your path to healing and recovery will be successful...

Should you have any comments or have questions you need answered, you can reach me at Linda0331@icloud.com.

Namaste.....

Linda M. Price, Ph.D., Psychotherapist

REFERENCES

Gottman, John M.,PhD. The Seven Principles for Making

Marriage Work, 1999, 2015, Harmony Books, New York, pages 31-51

Chapman, Gary D., The Five Love Languages, (Chicago:

Northfield Publishing, 1992, 1995, 2004, 2010)